Date: 9/24/15

J BIO EDISON
Yasuda, Anita,
Thomas Edison /

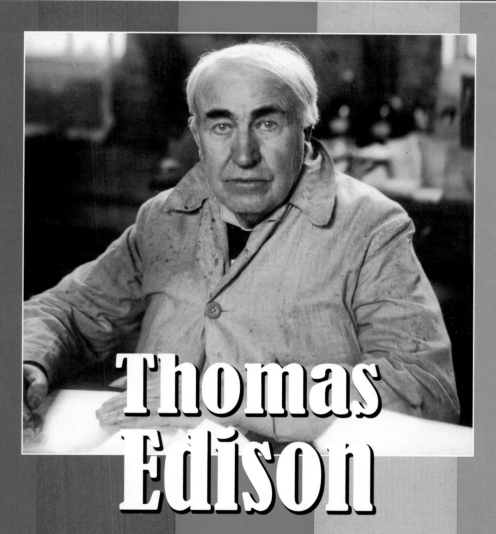

Thomas Edison

by Anita Yasuda

AV² provides enriched content that supplements and complements this book. Weigl's AV² books strive to create inspired learning and engage young minds in a total learning experience.

Your AV² Media Enhanced books come alive with...

Audio
Listen to sections of the book read aloud.

Key Words
Study vocabulary, and complete a matching word activity.

Video
Watch informative video clips.

Quizzes
Test your knowledge.

Go to **www.av2books.com**, and enter this book's unique code.

BOOK CODE

Y372468

Embedded Weblinks
Gain additional information for research.

Slide Show
View images and captions, and prepare a presentation.

AV² by Weigl brings you media enhanced books that support active learning.

Try This!
Complete activities and hands-on experiments.

... and much, much more!

Published by AV² by Weigl
350 5th Avenue, 59th Floor
New York, NY 10118

www.av2books.com   www.weigl.com

Editor: Megan Cuthbert
Design: Tammy West

Photograph Credits
Weigl acknowledges Getty Images as the primary image supplier for this title. Every reasonable effort has been made to trace ownership and to obtain permission to reprint copyright material. The publishers would be pleased to have any errors or omissions brought to their attention so that they may be corrected in subsequent printings.

Library of Congress Control Number: 2013953169

ISBN 978-1-4896-0636-5 (hardcover)
ISBN 978-1-4896-0637-2 (softcover)
ISBN 978-1-4896-0638-9 (Multi-user eBook)
ISBN 978-1-4896-0639-6 (Single-user eBook)

Printed in the United States of America in North Mankato, Minnesota
1 2 3 4 5 6 7 8 9 0 18 17 16 15 14

WEP301113
122013

Contents

Who Was Thomas Edison?

Thomas Edison was a famous **inventor**. He created many machines and tools that helped improve people's lives. Most of his inventions are still used today. Some of Thomas's best-known inventions include the **phonograph**, a movie projector called a **kinetoscope**, and the **incandescent** light bulb.

People relied on gas lamps, candles, and fireplaces to provide light at home. In 1879, Thomas created a long-burning electric light. To achieve this, he attached a strip of paper to wires within a glass bulb. When electricity flowed through the wires, the bulb glowed. Soon, Thomas's electric lights and lighting system would be used throughout the world.

Thomas believed that hard work would lead to success. Sometimes, his experiments did not work as planned. He did not consider them failures. Instead, he felt that he was getting closer to a solution.

"Many of life's failures are people who did not realize how close they were to success when they gave up."

Growing Up

Thomas Alva Edison was born February 11, 1847, in Milan, Ohio. Thomas's father, Samuel Edison, Jr., worked at many different jobs, including one job as an innkeeper. Thomas's mother Nancy was a former schoolteacher.

As a young child, Thomas was curious about the world around him. He enjoyed visiting the canal near his home, which was a hub of activity. When he was seven, Thomas's family moved to Port Huron, Michigan. Thomas was fascinated by the town's **miller**, who was trying to build a hot air balloon that could hold passengers.

Sometimes, Thomas's curiosity led to accidents. Thomas once fell inside a large grain elevator. Another time, he set his father's barn on fire. At school, one of Thomas's teachers labeled him a slow learner. Nancy disagreed, and she began teaching Thomas herself. She encouraged Thomas to read a variety of books. Science interested Thomas. He wanted to understand how things worked. Thomas soon set up a chemistry lab in his home.

◀ The house where Thomas born was turned into a museum. The Edison Birthplace Museum opened in Milan, Ohio, in 1947, 100 years after Thomas's birth.

Get to Know Ohio

SCALE
0   50 Miles
0   50 Kilometers

N

PENNSYLVANIA

OHIO

INDIANA

WEST VIRGINIA

In 1803, Ohio became the 17th state to join the United States of America.

Columbus is the capital of Ohio. The city is home to the Ohio General Assembly, which is the state's legislature building.

The state motto is "With God all things are possible."

The word Ohio comes from an **Iroquois** word meaning "great river."

STATE SYMBOLS

TREE
Ohio Buckeye

BIRD
Cardinal

FLOWER
Carnation

Practice Makes Perfect

At age 12, Thomas went to work for the Grand Trunk Railroad. He sold newspapers, dime-novels, and candy on the train as it traveled along the Port Huron-to-Detroit line. This was an exciting job as the railroad in the United States was still new.

▲ A statue of young Thomas Edison stands near the St. Clair River in Port Huron, Michigan.

In 1862, Thomas bought a used printing press. While he was working for the Grand Trunk Railroad, he began writing and printing a newspaper called *The Weekly Herald*. He also set up a **laboratory** in an empty baggage car. Thomas enjoyed experimenting aboard the train in his spare time. One day, an accident in his lab caused a fire to break out. It was the end of both Thomas's mobile printing press and his lab. On another occasion, Thomas rescued the son of a station master from being run down by a freight train. The boy's father offered to teach Thomas railroad **telegraphy** as a reward. Telegraphy was considered state-of-the art **telecommunications** at the time.

By the age of 16, Thomas was working as a telegraph operator in Port Huron. Over the next few years, Thomas took telegraph jobs in Canada and the United States.

QUICK FACTS

- Thomas Alva Edison's boyhood nickname was Al.
- Thomas's thousands of inventions earned him the nickname, "The Wizard of Menlo Park."
- Thomas created the first strand of Christmas lights.

◀ Telegraph machines used electric wires to transmit messages across the country. Telegraphers had to send and receive messages, as well as maintain the equipment.

Key Events

In 1868, Thomas created an electrical vote counter. The machine was meant to speed up the voting process. Unfortunately, the United States Congress was not interested in his invention. It preferred the traditional method of voting, and Thomas failed to sell it. Thomas did not give up. Instead, he decided to focus his attention on machines that would sell.

In 1876, Thomas set up a laboratory in Menlo Park, New Jersey. He nicknamed it the "Invention Factory." Thomas hired people who had the skills he needed to bring his inventions to life. The same year, Edison improved upon Alexander Graham Bell's telephone. The technology he invented produced a signal that could be heard more clearly.

It was during these experiments that Thomas began thinking of ways to record telephone conversations. He developed a machine that used a grooved metal cylinder to make a recording. This was the phonograph. Thomas thought businesses would use the phonograph to dictate letters. Instead, it was mostly used by people to play music.

▲ Thomas's good friend Henry Ford recreated the Menlo Park laboratory from old photographs. It can be viewed at the Henry Ford Museum and Greenfield Village in Michigan.

Thoughts from Thomas

Thomas Edison believed that hard work was essential in order to achieve goals. Here are a few of his comments on work and inventing.

Thomas talks about the future of electricity.

"Electricity is undoubtedly destined to be a great blessing to mankind: one of the greatest, if not absolutely the greatest force in the universe."

Thomas believed in the importance of perseverance.

"Genius is one percent inspiration and 99 percent perspiration."

Thomas explains the difference between being an inventor and a scientist.

"A scientific man busies himself with a theory. An inventor is essentially practical... As soon as I find that something I am investigating does not lead to practical results, I do not pursue it as a theory."

Thomas talks about which invention he enjoyed working on the most.

"The phonograph: I had a lot of fun with that...the development of the phonograph was most interesting."

Thomas explains the difference between a discovery and an invention.

"Discovery is not invention, and I dislike to see the two words confounded. A discovery is more or less in the nature of an accident."

Thomas believed in moving forward.

"...I'm 67 years old...but I'm none too old to take a fresh start tomorrow morning. Nobody is ever too old to take a fresh start."

What Is an Inventor?

Inventors are creative people. They think of original and useful ideas. Sometimes, they work in teams. Inventors often have backgrounds in engineering, medicine, or another science. Thomas Edison did not have a formal education. He furthered his knowledge through reading and experimenting. Today, many inventors go to school. They may study engineering or computer science.

Inventors have to first identify a problem. They think about various solutions and experiment in order to solve problems. Experiments allow inventors to know if their design works and what changes they must apply in order to fix it. Becoming an inventor takes hard work and dedication. Inventors work long hours and perform many tests and experiments. It often takes many years before an inventor successfully creates an invention.

▶ **Thomas worked with a group of assistants when creating his inventions.**

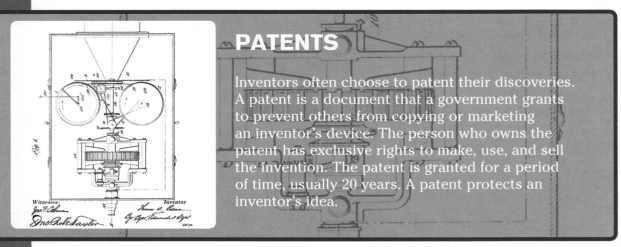

PATENTS

Inventors often choose to patent their discoveries. A patent is a document that a government grants to prevent others from copying or marketing an inventor's device. The person who owns the patent has exclusive rights to make, use, and sell the invention. The patent is granted for a period of time, usually 20 years. A patent protects an inventor's idea.

Famous Inventors 101

Nikola Tesla (1856-1943)

Nikola Tesla was born in July, 1856. He came to the United States in 1884. Nikola developed an alternating-current (AC) machine, which changed the way electricity was transferred. Nikola's AC system is still the standard electric power system in the world. He also invented the Tesla Coil. It is still used today in radio and television sets. In 1895, Tesla designed the first hydroelectric power plant, at Niagara Falls, in the United States.

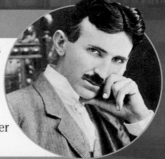

Henry Ford (1863-1947)

Henry Ford was born on July 30, 1863, near Dearborn, Michigan. From an early age, he was fascinated by machines. Ford was very interested in building a horseless carriage. In 1896, he completed his first self-propelled vehicle. Henry Ford formed the Ford Motor Company on June 16, 1903. He built the Model T in 1908. The Model T was the first affordable car.

Alexander Graham Bell (1847-1922)

Alexander Graham Bell was born in Edinburgh, Scotland, in March, 1847. It was while he was teaching the deaf that Alexander thought of building a microphone. Later, he made an "electrical speech machine," which became known as the telephone. On March 7, 1876, Alexander received a patent for his invention of sending a simple current over a wire. A few days later, he sent his own voice over the wire.

Steve Jobs (1955-2011)

Steve Jobs was born on February 24, 1955, in San Francisco, California. As a young child, he enjoyed working on electronics with his father. In 1976, Steve Jobs and Steve Wozniak started Apple Computers. Together, they changed the computer business by making computers smaller and more affordable.

Influences

Thomas's earliest influences were his mother and father. Though he attended school briefly in Port Huron, his basic education came from his mother Nancy. Thomas would later say that his mother was his biggest champion. Nancy encouraged Thomas to read. He felt that he had to work hard so as not to disappoint her.

Thomas's father, Samuel, held a variety of jobs. He worked in the lumber business and in **land speculation**. Samuel taught Thomas the importance of business. As an adult, Thomas would form businesses to manufacture and market his inventions.

▲ An exhibit in the Thomas Edison Depot Museum, in Port Huron, shows the support Thomas's mother gave him as a child.

After leaving home to work on the railroad, Thomas discovered the work of British scientist Michael Faraday. Faraday had discovered that metal vibrations could be converted to electrical currents. Thomas read Faraday's research at the public library. Faraday's experiments with electricity impressed Thomas. He applied this new knowledge to his own work.

THE EDISON FAMILY

Thomas married his first wife, Mary Stilwell, in 1871. She had worked for him in New Jersey. The couple had three children. Marion was born in 1873, followed by Thomas, Jr. in 1876, and William Leslie in 1878. Thomas nicknamed his older children "Dot" and "Dash" after telegraphic terms. Mary died in 1884. Two years later, Thomas married Mina Miller. They had three children. Madeline was born in 1888, Charles in 1890, and Theodore in 1898.

▲ Thomas's son, Charles, worked alongside his father at Thomas A. Edison, Incorporated. In 1927, Charles became president of the company.

Overcoming Obstacles

When Thomas began working for the railroad, he was almost completely deaf. No one knows for certain why this happened. Thomas could hear some sounds, but he had to pay close attention to what was going on around him because he could no longer rely on only his hearing. Thomas claimed that his deafness gave him an advantage because he could not hear the distractions around him.

In 1877, Thomas began working on an electric light system. Other people were working on electric lights too, but they used electric arc lighting. Arc lights are very bright, so they were mostly used outdoors. The lights were not very effective, however. If one light burned out, all the lights stopped working.

▲ One of Thomas's main competitors was Joseph W. Swan. The two eventually formed a company together, the Edison & Swan United Electric Company.

▲ Thomas later created a light bulb that could last up to 1,200 hours. The bulb contained a bamboo filament.

Thomas wanted to solve this problem. From 1878 to 1879, he tested more than 1,600 types of materials for the wire inside the bulb. This wire, called a **filament**, gave off a glow when heated. After many failed experiments and tests, Thomas succeeded in developing an electric light bulb. Thomas's light bulb could burn for more than 13 hours. Over the next few years, Thomas and his team worked on a system to deliver electricity. They developed a system that used wires, fuses, and switches. People could light their homes with electric light bulbs instead of gas lamps.

Achievements and Successes

By 1882, Thomas had built the first public power station in New York City. His system was capable of lighting 25 buildings. In 1887, Thomas set up the Edison General Electric Company.

Thomas and his staff began working on a motion picture camera in 1888. Thomas called the machine a kinetoscope. *Kineto* is Greek for "movement." *Scopos* means "to watch." Thomas's kinetoscope was a large wooden box with a peephole. People looked through the hole and saw a moving picture. Within a few years, people were paying money at kinetoscope parlors to see motion pictures.

In 1914, when Thomas was 67 years old, fire destroyed his factory in New Jersey. Thomas quickly rebuilt the factory. He continued working on his inventions. His last experiments involved trying to find a substitute for rubber.

◀ **Thomas's kinetoscope works by feeding a strip of photographs past a magnifying lens, which projects the images. The strips of photographs, or reels, are projected quickly, to give the appearance of movement.**

In 1928, the United States Congress awarded Thomas the **Congressional gold medal**. When Thomas Edison died in 1931, President Hoover suggested that the nation turn off its electric lights in honor of Thomas. In 1973, Thomas became the first inventor inducted into the National Inventors Hall of Fame and Museum.

HELPING OTHERS

In the years before his death, Thomas Edison sponsored scholarships for outstanding high school students. Candidates were selected through a national contest. Eligible students had to write a test at Edison's lab in New Jersey. Today, the Edison Innovation Foundation, a nonprofit organization that was set up in memory of the inventor, encourages students to pursue careers in science, technology, and engineering.

▲ Thomas's scholarships were meant to help students further their education. After winning the scholarship, the recipients were able to meet Thomas in person.

Write a Biography

A person's life story can be the subject of a book. This kind of book is called a biography. Biographies describe the lives of remarkable people, such as those who have achieved great success or have done important things to help others. These people may be alive today, or they may have lived many years ago. Reading a biography can help you learn more about a remarkable person.

At school, you might be asked to write a biography. First, decide who you want to write about. You can choose an inventor, such as Thomas Edison, or any other person. Then, find out if your library has any books about this person. Learn as much as you can about him or her. Write down the key events in this person's life. What was this person's childhood like? What has he or she accomplished? What are his or her goals? What makes this person special or unusual?

A concept web is a useful research tool. Read the questions in the following concept web. Answer the questions in your notebook. Your answers will help you write a biography.

Your Opinion

- What did you learn from the books you read in your research?
- Would you suggest these books to others?
- Was anything missing from these books?

Childhood

- Where and when was this person born?
- Describe his or her parents, siblings, and friends.
- Did this person grow up in unusual circumstances?

Adulthood

- Where does this individual currently reside?
- Does he or she have a family?

Writing a Biography

Main Accomplishments

- What is this person's life's work?
- Has he or she received awards or recognition for accomplishments?
- How have this person's accomplishments served others?

Work and Preparation

- What was this person's education?
- What was his or her work experience?
- How does this person work; what is or was the process he or she uses or used?

Help and Obstacles

- Did this individual have a positive attitude?
- Did he or she receive help from others?
- Did this person have a mentor?
- Did this person face any hardships?
- If so, how were the hardships overcome?

Timeline

YEAR	THOMAS EDISON	WORLD EVENTS
1847	Thomas Edison is born in Milan, Ohio.	The first United States telegraph company is established in Maryland.
1868	Thomas is awarded his first patent for the electric vote recorder, but no one buys it.	The very first traffic lights are installed in London, England.
1877	Thomas invents his first phonograph.	The first telephone is installed in Massachusetts.
1879	Thomas and his team successfully make a light bulb that lasts more than 13 hours.	A hearing aid called the Audiophone is invented by Richard Rhodes.
1882	Thomas opens the first commercial electric power station in the United States.	Henry W. Seely patents the electric iron.
1894	Thomas's kinetoscope parlor, in New York City, opens to the public.	A U.S. patent is awarded to Karl Benz for a gasoline-driven automobile.
1931	Thomas dies on October 18 in West Orange, New Jersey.	The Empire State Building opens in New York.

Key Words

Congressional gold medal: highest award in the United States for distinguished achievement

filament: a thin wire in a light bulb that glows when electricity passes through it

incandescent: contains a filament that emits light when heated

inventor: a person who creates something new such as a machine

Iroquois: American Indians that traditionally lived in New York State and southern Ontario and Quebec

kinetoscope: an early motion picture machine

laboratory: a place where experiments take place

land speculation: buying land in order to sell at a higher price

miller: a person who grinds corn or other crops at a mill

phonograph: a machine that records and plays sound

telecommunications: the exchange of information over a distance by electronics

telegraphy: the use of electrical impulses to send information over a wire

Index

Log on to www.av2books.com

AV² by Weigl brings you media enhanced books that support active learning. Go to www.av2books.com, and enter the special code found on page 2 of this book. You will gain access to enriched and enhanced content that supplements and complements this book. Content includes video, audio, weblinks, quizzes, a slide show, and activities.

AV² Online Navigation

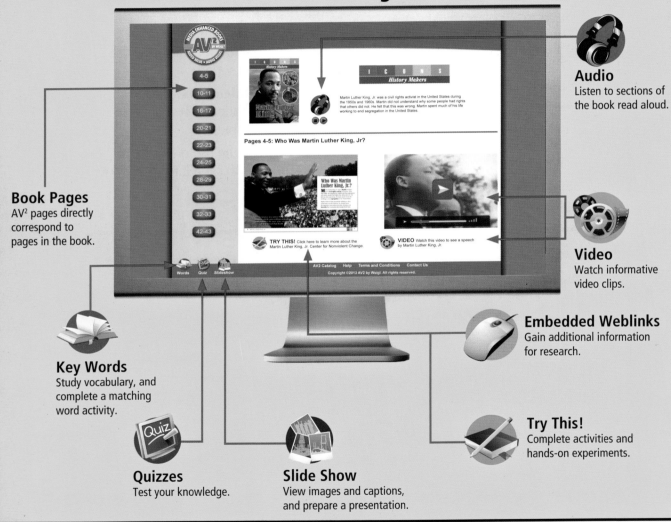

Audio
Listen to sections of the book read aloud.

Book Pages
AV² pages directly correspond to pages in the book.

Video
Watch informative video clips.

Embedded Weblinks
Gain additional information for research.

Key Words
Study vocabulary, and complete a matching word activity.

Try This!
Complete activities and hands-on experiments.

Quizzes
Test your knowledge.

Slide Show
View images and captions, and prepare a presentation.

AV² was built to bridge the gap between print and digital. We encourage you to tell us what you like and what you want to see in the future.

Sign up to be an AV² Ambassador at www.av2books.com/ambassador.